LIVE FREE

The
Eight Principles
to Improve
Your Income,
Relationships
and Life

LIVE
FREE

WILLIAM WILSON

ISBN : 9781693571091

Design: Heike Schüssler

Dedicated to my wife,
in whom loyalty
and trust merge to obtain
their meaning and existence
in the purest form.

CONTENTS

INTRODUCTION

This book has emerged as a result of my personal ambition to provide a concise way of answering basic questions asked by men. People live in their own individual realities that are also part of the common objective reality of the world we currently live in. Objective reality is a man's playground for expressing his individual reality. A man has the opportunity to develop his potential and gradually move to a higher level of existence. Depending on how fast we learn the lessons we are going through, this journey can be shorter or longer, at least viewed from the man's time perception. It is the duty of every man to become aware of his responsibility. Nothing simply happens to us. We are the ones who act, even by not acting at all. Our actions are not limited to body movements. There is a hidden world within us that is responsible for both luck and misfortune. Everything we experience, everything we do and what others do to us, is the reflection of our own world we keep within ourselves. I sincerely hope that this short book will provide certain insights to the person reading this that will serve as a basis for understanding himself and the world he temporarily exists in.

ABUNDANCE
IS EVERYWHERE

Abundance is all around us. All of nature is expressed in abundance. There is an infinite number of blades of grass, leaves on trees, snowflakes, and drops of water. Wherever you look, you will see abundance in nature. Existence manifests itself in countless ways and forms, in all directions, and according to clearly defined principles. These principles contain certain validities. Nature knows no limit in its expression. The only limitation is in our minds, in our thinking. Since childhood, we have been taught ourselves to believe that if we can't think of a way to get something right away, we can't have it at all. Then we stop looking for a way to get something, and so our desire dies before it can reach its potential.

All things come from the higher nature of existence, from the non-physical energy potential and into the physical material form. If we don't see something on the physical plane, we say it doesn't exist. Our eyes are able to see one frequency range, and the rest of the world is beyond that range. Even so, we believe that an imaginary car from our mind does not exist just because we don't see it in the frequency range that our eyes can translate into physical reality. There is an abundance of friends, an abundance of money, and an abundance of health. It's all around us. We just have to accept this fact even before we can see it with our physical eyes.

We are taught to believe only what we see, but that is not faith at all. To believe means to feel with the whole being, to see with the whole being. We see what we believe in. If we see an abundance of money in our minds and choose to focus on just one idea, we initiate the creative process that nature uses in the expression process and thus manifest from the potential energy into the actual physical form the thing we see in our minds. It is not necessary to limit ourselves to one form of wealth or one channel, for life is abundantly expressed in all forms and in all directions. The whole universe is an expression of the abundance of existence itself. Man as a conscious individual has every right to become the recipient and distributor of abundance. All one has to do is know the laws and apply them consciously in one's life.

EVERYTHING VIBRATES

It is a scientific fact that everything we see at its atomic level vibrates at a certain frequency. Our brains translate these frequencies and allow us to experience this world as a world of solid objects, although it is not. The nature of the body, mind, and dimension in which we temporarily exist as human beings is such that we see and feel as solid something that is not solid.

Since birth, we have been taught to believe that everything is firm. We can also feel when it's not. The nature of every physical form is the movement of energy. The whole universe is in constant motion. From the grain of sand to the star in the sky, everything has its own vibration frequency, and everything moves.

We can access anything by simply matching our own frequency with the frequency of the things we want. We can literally attract whatever we want if we match the vibration of our being with things in the present moment. Our feeling means vibration, and we vibrate and attract according to how we feel. If we feel negative emotions, we cannot attract anything positive into our lives. Negative emotions such as anger, depression, and sadness all have their own frequency, and they can only attract similar feelings.

You cannot expect heat unless you provide the wood. Life doesn't work that way. It is necessary to feel joy first so the events that cause you joy can happen in your life. Joy and happiness are within you, and you can produce them even when you have no reason for them. You can imagine in your mind things that will make you happy, such as buying a house. In the world of vibration, your feelings are the point of attraction. How you feel now determines what you will get later.

Outside things may inspire you to feel content, but it is not creation. It is the process of maintaining an existing state. So if your life is full of contentment and you are happy about your life, you will continue to feel happy because your life is content. Basically, first there was a happy feeling then a manifestation of a pleasant life, not the other way around. Every thought affects your emotions and the vibration of your body, so it is important that you keep your thoughts in check. If you think thoughts that are in line with your current results, you will have feelings that are in harmony with your results, and your actions will be in line with those feelings, leading to getting the same results again. This is how you keep going for almost your entire life without ever noticing it, and that's why it's important to surround yourself with the people who live the life you want.

Go to a nice hotel or a restaurant where you will feel beautiful. No matter your current results, do not spend a single moment in places where you don't feel happy or with people who don't think the way you do. Your world, which you keep in your mind, always gets its physical form through the laws of the universe. The fact that nobody sees it right now doesn't matter. What matters is what you see within you because you are the center through which existence is transformed from energy into form.

WHERE DOES IT ALL COME FROM?

The center of abundance from which all things originate is not a person who has an endless list of all the inhabitants on Earth with their desires and who works hard to deliver all our demands, both possible and impossible. It is a vibrational energy center that responds to the vibrations that come to it in every moment. It is not personal; it does not reward or punish us for our good and bad deeds respectively. It is the very nature of existence, a pure consciousness that does not speak our language. The only language it knows is the language of our feelings, and it responds to them in the same way. If you complain about not having enough money or about your children not being obedient, you are sending vibrations of a certain frequency into the cosmos. When your thoughts arrive at the center at a certain point, the center thinks you are looking for more of it. Since it loves you immensely, it gives you more of the same in many forms because it is creative and expresses itself abundantly. It sends you more money troubles, arranges for you to drop your wallet on the street, and sends you fines at your home address. The center is the intelligence of existence, and there is an infinite number of ways of manifesting it in all dimensions.

That is why it is important that you control your feelings no matter what you currently see in your life. What you see is yours and is your problem only. When you finally see the results, they are already past. There is nothing you can do about it. You can only accept them. If you complain about them arriving in a certain form, the universe, again, instantly receives new signals through vibration and starts delivering new content all over again. Many people do not understand this principle of life and continue to get the same results over and over again every year. They continue to complain about not having money, and they continue with the same actions that bring them the same results. Therefore, prayer in the form that most people experience it has no effect. They get more of the same.

When you kneel down and pray that God will give you something you do not already have, you will get even less of it because at the heart of such a prayer is the feeling and awareness of not having it. The universe is not your mother, who will jump to her feet as soon as you complain. Real prayer is what you do between prayers. Most people are not even aware of this. They don't know what they're doing to themselves and don't realize everything has its own frequency. Every tree, blade of grass, stone, and grain of sand, as well as your finger on your hand, the money in your wallet, and your wallet itself, has its own frequency. We live in a vibrating universe, and our nervous system translates these vibrations into objects that we can see, feel, smell, and hear. Therefore, when we look at an object under a special microscope, we do not see the object but rather tiny energy particles moving at an enormous speed. With the help of the instrument, we see the true nature of each object: That it is not a static thing but a movement of energy.

The only way to get a certain thing or experience is by stepping into its frequency. Imagine an endless number of highways in the sky stretching in all directions. To get a certain thing in your life, you have to find yourself on the same highway as that particular thing. You will never get that desired thing if you look at it from the ground and simply pray that it comes to you. You have to change your height (frequency) and climb toward it, and you do this through your focus and feelings. What you look at, you get. That is why it is very important to control your feelings when looking at your results and to keep in mind who you are paying attention to. Your attention is your creative center. Everything, seen and unseen, is already in the center of abundance in its energetic form. Man has the ability to turn energy into shape. Man already does it, whether he knows it or not.

PRINCIPLE 1:
Imagine & Manifest
Your Results

Imagination is one of our innate virtues that needs to be further developed, just like memory, intuition, thinking, will-power, and perception. Imagination is our creative force. Through visualization, we have the power to convert any energy into form. That is our natural ability. That is why humans are the co-creators of the world they belong to. Imagination is our connection with the higher dimensions of nature. Through visualization, we are mentally moving into a creative dimension, which is energetic in nature by its vibration and is above the physical realm we live in. Everything is created first in the mind through visualization, which we call imagination. Everything you see around you is an expression of this power.

But we don't just create physical objects that we can perceive. Our whole life is created out of imagination and so are the events that we participate in, even though we are not aware of it. The reason why we do not recognize the connection between a particular event and our imagination is because of the speed of manifestation. It is impossible to create something as soon as we imagine it. That would not be in harmony with life. Imagine what life would be like if children started manifesting the things they see in their minds and adults manifested their desires instantly. You live as you think. We're talking about ingrained thoughts, which have already been formed as attitudes. True creation is the focus of our thoughts on a particular thing or event, with the feeling that it is already fulfilled. All you can do is plant the idea in the subconscious; everything else happens automatically. Imagination and feeling are creation, so the ultimate question for you is: How would you feel if you had what you want right now? If I had that car now, how would I feel? If I had that house now, how would I feel? If I had kids now, how would I feel?

Determine the answers to these questions, and start feeling that way now. Feeling is a manifestation, so practice these feelings every day. Ask yourself a question and produce a feeling. Try to follow each imagining with the feeling you would have. At the core of our every desire lies a beautiful feeling. We want to feel good, and we are taught to only feel good when we have the things we want. So we need to turn this process around in a creative way. Let's feel happy first in order to bring the things and experiences we want into our lives. This feeling is a direct order to your subconscious to create these in your world. The subconscious has no ability to reject the idea but only to execute the idea presented in the form of feelings. That is why it is very important to keep an eye on your feelings and moods as only these can be manifested.

Where do most people go wrong? They want one thing in the conscious part of their mind, but in the subconscious, they feel that bad things will happen. The conscious part of the mind does not affect the vibration, only the subconscious part does, and therefore their desires and hopes are never fulfilled unless they are accompanied by that particular feeling of elation that occurs at the level of the subconscious.

Ask yourself over and over how you would feel if you had a new car or a new house or if you were completely healthy. Practice that feeling every day while exercising your imagination. According to the law of the universe, this exact same scene from your imagination must be transformed into your physical equivalent. As Einstein said, God did not roll the dice with the universe. All of life works according to clearly defined laws. All we have to do is consciously apply the laws in our lives. The energy in the form of thoughts in your imagination is exactly the same energy that now takes shape in your life as a new car. Thoughts about the car and the car come from the same energy that vibrates differently, so one moment that car is just a thought and the next it is the physical form in the shape of the car that we can see in front of us. The only difference is in the level of vibration of that energy. It is our job to learn to change this vibration of thoughts into its physical form.

HOW TO APPLY IMAGINATION

Now you are sitting in New York, in your living room, and you would like to travel to London for the New Year, but you do not have enough money. Instead of being desperate because you have no money, imagine you are physically sitting in London at this very moment. Close your eyes and imagine yourself sitting in a chair at a hotel by the window. You watch people walk down the street in a hurry. You see snowflakes making their way to the ground and a black cab going down the street. You see a man stopping a taxi. Just think about your apartment in New York and think about how things are in New York at this very moment. Mentally go through the rooms of your apartment in New York. You are now in London thinking of New York. Stay in this scene long enough, in a hotel room in London, until it takes the form of reality for you now. Touch the chair with your mental hands, touch the curtains, and look at the welcome card with your last name on it on the table next to you.

Get out on the street mentally. Go to the store. Buy what you would buy if you were there now. Practice this exercise 30 days in a row, every night when you go to sleep.

Your subconscious, which is the creative force of your mind, cannot differentiate between an imagined scene and a scene that is happening, because for your subconscious, both scenes are happening now, and everything is real. That's why when you watch movies, actors can make you happy or sad — your subconscious can't tell the difference. That scene, repeated often enough in your mind, gives the order to your subconscious to draw that same scene into your life as reality. Always concentrate on the end result only. Don't try to think of ways to get what you want, because your ideas are based only on past experiences and, as such, limit the creative force of the universe, which knows an infinite number of methods. Just as there is an abundance of money, so there are endless ways for that money to come into your possession.

If you want to buy a new car, choose the car you would like to own. Now that you have that car in your garage, what do you think about it? Create an ideal scene in your imagination that involves using that car or that involves buying a new car at a dealership. Imagine buying it and the seller congratulating you on your purchase. Get in the car and grab the wheel. Touch the leather on the seats. Can you smell the new car smell? Neville Goddard said, "If a rose does not exist, why is its scent in the air?" Apply the same rule to your car when you think it is not realistic. It is as realistic as anything else you can see around you now. Enjoy it. Drive it, give your friend a ride, and see your friend being happy because you bought a new car. Repeat this scene until the rain falls and until it comes to fruition. The moment you imagine it, you have created that car for yourself, just not in this vibration level, which your physical eyes can see. But you can see it with your mental eyes because it is on another vibration frequency range. If you continue to create this same scene in your mind long enough, you will accelerate the formation of that scene on the material plane.

Each physical seed has its own growth period. The same is true of spiritual seeds as well. When you imagine your car, you are planting a spiritual seed, and it is only a matter of time before it will be born in your world. It is the law of existence. Hope and desire are not the same as belief. They remain at the conscious level of the mind. But what you see in your world depends on what you feel at the subconscious level. You have to believe because belief is a specific feeling that guarantees manifestation. Believing is matching the frequency of the thing you believe in.

Believing is knowing. You are not simply hoping to get this thing — you already have it. The feeling that must be produced in the imagination is the feeling of complete conviction that you now have what you are imagining because only with that feeling can you access the power of the subconscious, which will give you everything you need to achieve on the physical level what you see on the mental level in your mind. Feeling is a vibration. Your actions must always be consistent with the vibration your body is in. We get reactions to our actions that produce results. That is why our only task is to use the good feeling to insert into the subconscious the images we want to manifest. It's also the only thing we can do — to feel good no matter what the circumstances are now.

Circumstances are always the product of past feelings, not the other way around. If you have something in your life now that you do not love, you need to be aware that you have produced that condition in the past through your feelings, whether it is poverty or illness. In fact, every illness first begins in our minds. Nothing happens on a physical level. This world we live in is an absolute creation created in the minds of individuals. The physical world is a world of consequences, not causes. That's why you can't change anything if you look at what you already are. By looking at what you are, you create more of what you are. That is why it is necessary to turn to your imagination to see a perfect life in your mind. Whenever things in life are not the way you want them to be, remember that your imagination is a creative power. It is the negative feelings and moods that brought you to those undesirable results in the first place.

Let's say you want more money. You have a stack of bills to pay, and you feel that nothing in your life is changing for the better. You see a bill you don't know how to pay, and you know that more bills are coming, so you start worrying out of habit. Worrying produces restlessness. Since the universe is not personal, it gives you more in relation to the vibe you are in. Stop looking at what you are but imagine the final outcome as you wish it was now. How would you feel if you paid all the bills now, bought that car, or paid for that trip? You would feel relief. Feel that relief now if you want to see it in your life. You don't need a single thing from this world to change your mood, which is the basis of creation. Your world is inside, not outside. The cause of all the conditions you witness is within you. You don't need money to feel rich. Wealth is a state of mind and has nothing to do with money.

Wealth is abundance, and money is only one form of it. If you need the money to feel good, you will always be in trouble because you are doing the opposite of the laws that keep your entire existence in order. Feel good first to see the money in your life. Imagine saying, "Give me a fire, and I'll give you some wood." You have to give the wood first to get the heat. You must first see in your mind the state you want and produce the feeling that goes with that state to witness that state from the outside. It is a creation because everything proceeds from higher to lower. The energy of creation goes from a higher dimension of nature to a lower one. The physical world is a world of consequence. Nothing new emerges in it. So you must first see in your imagination what you want to see in your world. Plant the seed and relax. By the laws of nature and life, this must be accomplished.

When you feel happy after your imagining is over, then you will know that what you regularly imagine will come to you. When you are imagining, you are in the vibration of the things you imagine.

HOW I BOUGHT MY FIRST CAR

A few years ago, I began to consciously apply my imagination in my life. Having grown up in an environment where having a Mercedes is a very big deal, I decided to try out if imagination works. I imagined a few scenes that would otherwise happen if I owned a Mercedes. As soon as I woke up in the morning, I would start to imagine driving a new Mercedes. I would see the steering wheel in my hands and imagine the landscapes I would travel through. When I would ride on a bus, I imagined sitting in my Mercedes. When I showered, I would drive a Mercedes. I also often imagined the scene of buying a Mercedes. I envisioned one model I loved, and I would buy that model again every day in my mind. I did these scenes every day for a few months. My imagination was very vivid and realistic. Basically, I persisted in this exercise. I put up a picture of a Mercedes in my room. Wherever I would look in that direction, I would always see that car.

I never uttered words like, "One day I'll buy, drive, and have," because that's the vibe of not having it. I would remind myself that I have one now, and I would do a brief imagining. After a few months, there was nothing happening in the way of finances or the arrival of the Mercedes. I didn't even know how I was going to buy it. If I had known, I probably would have bought one. The way I was going to get it was not for me to worry about. I was focused on the end result. The price of the new model was way higher than what I was earning at the time since I wasn't earning much. Still, I persisted in practicing imagination. I performed some scenes so well that after a while I began to feel joy when I was in my "imaginary" Mercedes.

I did not share this with anyone, because their reality would bring me back to the old way of thinking that I could not achieve it. No one in my area had a new car, especially a Mercedes, so it didn't make sense to tell anyone what I was doing. After a year, my friend then came suddenly with a job offer, which I accepted. After a few more months, we started making enough money to buy a Mercedes. One day we visited a car showroom, and I saw a Mercedes that met the criteria I had imagined. It wasn't the model I had imagined, but as soon as I sat in it, I saw a scene from my imagination. I was vibrationally ready for that car, and so I bought it.

I soon experienced many scenes with it that I had seen so many times in my imagination. I was not wondering how I was going to buy the thing I was imagining. I didn't doubt the scenes I had rehearsed. I remained disciplined and true to the image I saw in my mind, regardless of the opposite reality at the time. For months, there was no indication that I was going to buy that car, but I had been practicing for so long that it was no longer a question of whether it would appear and when. It became a part of my consciousness for me; it was real even before others could see it.

HOW I BOUGHT MY FIRST APARTMENT

Before I bought my first apartment, I determined the characteristics of the apartment itself. I spent several months searching for just such an apartment. It had to have a spacious living room and several rooms, with a few bathrooms and a nice view, and it had to be new and of a good construction quality. Whenever I looked at an apartment from an ad, there was always something missing. When I finally found the apartment I wanted, I had one problem: I didn't have enough money for that apartment. However, that did not discourage me. As soon as I entered that apartment, I toured all the rooms and already felt that I was in the vibration of that apartment. In the same building, I looked at several other similar apartments, but this one was special. Although I couldn't make an offer right away, I decided that particular apartment was mine. I went home and started imagining that same day that the apartment was already mine. Although I was short by a lot of money, I did not give up on the intention of owning this apartment. In the morning, when I woke up, I would imagine with my eyes closed the room in the new apartment. I would let the walls of my new apartment surround me. Then I would get up and wash myself in the new bathroom. I would go to the kitchen and make coffee for myself and my wife. Holding my coffee in my hand, I would stand in the living room, by the large window, watching people outside. I continued to imagine these and many other scenes on a regular basis every day. I did not let the awareness regarding the lack of money affect my mood. My goal was to create awareness during the imagining that I now had enough money and that I had already bought that apartment. After a few months, for some reason, the price of the apartment was lower than when I first saw it, and I started to earn more. After exactly eight months, I bought that apartment. Other apartments in that building had already been sold, but this one was waiting for me.

Whenever you want something, you have to create the awareness that you already have it, and that is how you should walk during the day. You can't imagine having something and then act the opposite. If you want to become a millionaire, walk like a millionaire before millions reach your account. Look like a millionaire, dress like a millionaire, and act like a millionaire.

PRINCIPLE 2:
Why the Law of Attraction Works for You Now

Bearing in mind what has been said so far, it is good to look back at the specific situations that permeate our daily lives. Most of us would love to be or have something more than what we are or have now. It is part of our innate tendency to develop.

If you want something, all you need to do is bring your being to a state of peace and use your innate virtues to accomplish your goal. Don't knock, don't ask, don't look for, and don't demand anything from anyone. We are not dealing with people; we are dealing with the universe. Relax and allow yourself to imagine the perfect scene in your mind, where what you want now is fulfilled. In doing so, you come to the same vibration level with the things you want, and those things will come to your life and experience.

◆ ◆ ◆

The Law of Attraction says that all that is happening to you now is a product of what you thought in the past. The past doesn't have to be that long ago. It is possible that yesterday you were talking about something with a lot of emotions and that you are witnessing this event today. There is no time in the universe as we experience it, and everything is happening right now. When we pay attention to an event, that event is already moving toward us. In fact, the object or event is already there on the physical plane, but it needs to be adjusted to the level of our vibration before we see it. Before you talked about it, you weren't aware of it, even when you walked past it down the street. The moment you pay attention to it, you suddenly open your awareness to the subject, and it begins to pop out in front of you from all sides. This simple rule applies for your entire life. When you start keeping a journal of your emotions and start paying attention to what you talk about with the people you meet during the day, you will realize that you are the master of creating your own reality. You are that top attractor.

This is not philosophy. Think about it: You are responsible for your entire life. You can't blame anyone. It's not your parents, your kids, or your friends who bear the blame; it's you. Everything that is happening to you has already happened to you inside, in your mind. Any fear you have will sooner or later be found in your physical reality and will come as a random unwanted guest. Any aspirations and intentions you keep hidden inside will sooner or later take shape in this reality because that is the law. Energy always flows into form. All you think is energy. If energy takes shape, it proves to us that thought takes shape, whether it is fear or a red Ferrari. In the end, the Ferrari is simply a thought on a higher dimension. The only reason you refuse to accept these facts is because you do not understand how the world you live in works. It may be that you never even thought about the things you are experiencing now, but these things have the same level of vibration as the topics that you were emotionally involved in earlier, and that is why the universe is now abundantly expressing itself and giving you back different experiences — the same energetic vibrations you sent first.

You do not even need to imagine a specific scene or outcome; you need only to feel a specific emotion for a certain amount of time.

Let's say something you have never imagined before happened to you. Suddenly you have a toothache, and after an appointment at the dentist's office, you find out that what is going on in your mouth requires surgery. Who would imagine that? But the emotions you have been feeling so strongly could have caused the disruption in your cells that gave you this outcome. Certain illnesses take approximately a year to manifest into the physical body if the emotions are strong and continual, like anger or sadness. The body is an instrument of the mind.

This is the main reason many people fail to recognise the results, because they could not find a link between the thoughts and the results.

APPLYING THIS LAW IN YOUR RELATIONSHIPS

Don't pray for things you don't want. Don't talk about them. Don't tell your friend how all girls are bad or all guys are bad. Once you say that and release that emotion, the only things you will find are girls and guys like that. Maybe until now you have been talking negatively about what you have been wanting for so long and life still provides you with the results of your past thoughts, but today you can change it.

First, be what you demand of others. We have some strange need to demand from others what we ourselves are Depending on the culture he lives in, he has different ideas of what perfect means. For some people, perfect means being obedient, and for someone else, it means being free and yourself. Perfect does not exist, no matter how much we aspire to this ideal. Our lives and all relationships have constant growth and development. Our relationship with our partner reflects our level of development as a person. The more we expand our awareness and understand ourselves, the more we understand the people around us. If we understand the needs we have, we can easily assume that the people we have relationships with have the same needs.

The basic aspiration of every person is to be free. Unfortunately, in most cases, the basic relationship between partners is not a relationship but an ownership. This is a game of energy, and whoever has the stronger energy becomes the owner of the other, while the other becomes the victim. If you want the perfect partner, you first need to understand your needs and your shortcomings and by no means look for a supplement in a partner. Your partner is a person just like you. If you want freedom for yourself, give that freedom to your partner first. If you want more free time, give more free time to your partner. Whatever you require from your partner, be that first.

Opposites are said to attract, but I don't think opposites can ever be attracted permanently. They can be touched briefly but never held together. If your thoughts and beliefs differ completely from that of your partner, sooner or later, by the laws of being, you must be separated.

HOW TO ATTRACT YOUR PARTNER

Imagine an ideal person for you. Do not imagine a particular person but imagine what qualities that person should have. You would love for that person to always be in a good mood and smiling, to have a sense of humor, to be aware, to be able to lift the mood, to be fair in nature, to be financially secure and able to manage money, and to be healthy. Now create a scene in your mind where you and that person live in the here and now. How would you feel if you were traveling with that person now? In your imagination, think of laughing together, making dinner, walking in the parks of London, and dancing. Imagine the best you can. Do not put a face to this person but only focus on the other features. You have yet to attract that person. Remember that this is a world of vibrations, that we are basically vibrational beings, and that everything works by frequency tuning.

When you think of a particular scene that suits you, repeat this exercise daily, as many times as possible. Put all your focus on it, and leave the universe to do its job. Do not push or force people or events. Everything works perfectly and simply in the universe without any effort. Rain and snow fall effortlessly, grass grows when the time is right, and all of this is expressed in abundance. This is what your life in all fields should look like, an absolute manifestation of effortlessness. The only thing you can do in your mind is focus your attention on a particular scene. Everything else will happen without you and according to the laws of the universe.

Many people want the perfect woman, but they constantly tell their friends that women are negative or toxic and that they do not understand them. You can't ask the universe for one thing and then look for the opposite of it the next moment. This is exactly what most people do. They consciously want one thing and subconsciously have views that contradict that thing. That is why the thing that they want in their life never actually manifests but only what they think deep inside does. It's the same with a partner, with money, and with health. People want money, work for it, and at the same time talk about money as the source of all evil, thus simply giving energy to what is already in their life and getting more of it. Our desires are in the conscious mind, but they do not affect the vibration the body is in. Our attitudes and ideas are in the subconscious, and they affect feelings, which is another word for vibration. This vibration affects the action that we get the reaction, that is, the results, from. Thus we realize that only what we feel deeply about everything can be seen in our lives.

That is why it is important to recognize what we think of a particular topic and remove it from us completely so that we no longer pay attention to it. Don't talk negatively about a partner, even though you haven't met him or her yet, and don't think negatively, because what you think is then happening in your life. Just think and talk positively. Find only the good in each person. Anyone can find the bad in someone, but to see the good in the bad takes effort. Direct all energy toward the final outcome, and let everything just happen automatically according to the laws. All of the manifested universe is manifested from spirit to matter. Nothing is created of matter first. Matter and all its events are merely products of the spirit. It's the same with a partner. That is why it is said, what is up is down. As in heaven, so on Earth.

You must first imagine in your mind (the heaven) the perfect partner and energize that scene long enough until it materializes. Each seed has its own growth period according to the law of gestation. The idea of a partner is a spiritual seed, which is the same as a physical seed. That spiritual seed has its growth period. The more you focus on the original scene in your mind by repeating that scene, the sooner it will materialize on the material plane in your life as an experience. This will happen suddenly, from an unexpected direction. Whenever we think, we think from previous experience, but often our experiences are limited by previous thinking, so we cannot assume all the channels the universe possesses when it comes to expressing abundance. This is why the right partner for you will come at a time when you are not expecting it, in a place you do not expect it to happen. You may think that the person in the cafe is the one or that the person you met at work is exactly the one you are imagining. The person who is the one sent to you by the universe, as a product of your focus, will be the person you will feel, because feeling is another word for vibration. You will simply know. It's a specific feeling. You just need to let it manifest when the time comes, not before it's time.

HOW TO KEEP SOMEONE YOU HAVE ATTRACTED

To keep anything you have requires a certain level of awareness. You need to work on yourself every day and make a habit of it. Read a good book that inspires you to make the best of what you have. Always be better than you were yesterday. Try to be as honest and as good as possible in your relationship. This is what you are, and no one can take it away from you. It is not about money or any other thing on the outside. It is about what you are on the inside.

If the person who is currently with you is unable to appreciate and respect the virtues and qualities that are unique to you, do not worry about it. The universe will send someone who is your perfect match. It is yours to give more and to be more. Always go one step further in your relationship. Be more tolerant and open. Put the needs of others before yours. Always use your behavior as an example to your partner for what you expect of him or her. In general, relationships between people are often difficult and require awareness and understanding of yourself first because when you understand yourself, then you can understand others.

PRINCIPLE 3:
Money Is a Result
of Your Service

Money is an idea that is expressed on a piece of paper, and we have agreed on its value. Money has no value outside our society. If you take money to an Amazon tribe, it will have no value at all to them. Money is inexhaustible in its nature because it is pure energy, and energy is infinite. The only limitation is in us. Our whole world is energy that is shaped into different forms that we perceive as objects. The same energy we call money, if we burn it, it will become ether or gas. Everything comes from one source, from the same energy. Money is everywhere. It is in and around us. Money is pure energy that can take shape in the physical world as soon as we invite it and accept it.

Maybe you can't buy happiness with money, but you can't buy anything with poverty. Just think about it. There is much more you can do with money than without it. In addition to making your life phenomenal, if you have money, you can help other people. You can set up foundations to help those who don't have it enough, and you can improve education in poor countries. The list is limitless.

Many people ignorantly say that money is not important. Although money is essentially energy, it plays an important role in our society. We exchange our time for the money we use to buy various things, such as clothes, food, or gas, or to pay a doctor. If we don't love money, it's because someone who didn't have it taught us not to love it. Everything you attach to it is your personal perception.

It has no meaning beyond its nature. Money is a tool for exchange and communication. You cannot attract money into your life if you think negatively about it. Would you go to a house of a person who hates you and speaks bad about you all the time but invites you to come anyway? You probably wouldn't. It's the same with money. On a conscious level, you want money because you need it, but deep down, you are taught to hate it. So you give a contradictory vibe to the universe, but only what is dominant, deep within you, counts for manifestation. Your deepest thoughts about everything can be seen in your life as an experience. This is the root cause of why you have or don't have something. Happiness and coincidence are not the causes. They are visible circumstances of invisible causes.

Lack of material interests is considered spirituality in some parts of the world. The lack of material interests is a misunderstanding of the nature of self and the nature of existence. We are already spiritually perfect. Here we are in an agreed upon self-forgetfulness to experience the lowest point of distance from God in all perfection that exists in the material sense. Matter and its entire physical world are the most obvious expression of spirituality, for all dimensions in existence arise from higher to lower. Therefore, in the divine manifestation, the material world is only the basest expression of the spiritual world. To say that someone is spiritual because he or she has no material interests is a linguistic paradox because there is no such thing. Being in the physical dimension itself, from object to person, is an expression of pure spirituality. Matter is made of spirit. To remain poor today is a sin and involves the unconscious maintenance of the inherited paradigm of those who, during our childhood, passed on their misperceptions to us in the form of attitudes and beliefs about money.

Money is as good as the one who owns and manages it. An evil man will always be evil, both with and without money. Money only has the ability to draw to the surface and magnify what a man has inside of him. If you are a good person, you will be even better if you have money.

◆ ◆ ◆

You need to change your perception of money if you want to attract it abundantly. Money has its own frequency, and we need to be at the same frequency if we want to attract it. How do we do this? By using our imagination and through visualization, we can imagine holding money in our hands, smell it, pay our bills, and buy clothes, a car, or a house. Use it in your imagination as much as possible. Since it is energy and your subconscious cannot differentiate the real from the imagined, it must produce an environment consistent with the images you create. Whether this energy will come into your possession is up to you. It will come and will continue to come if you learn to control it. Money, like all energy, loves to circulate. Movement is the nature of energy. Money must not stand in one place, waiting for the bad days to be used. Money needs to be invested to multiply. The universe is abundance. It is the source of innumerable money.

The only limit is in you because you are still thinking about having as much as you did last month. You keep this pattern of behavior all your life, and that's exactly how much you have. Somewhere deep inside of us is written how much we can have. That's almost a fixed number. No matter how much you would like to have money, no matter how hard you work, you cannot attract more than is written in you. It is a gift that you were given very early in your childhood, and it is related to your observations. If your parents had little money, chances are they taught you to have little money as well. It is almost certain that they taught you to do even the same job as them as your sole source of income. Everything you know about money is learned while growing up. Kids are great mimics. They copy behavior patterns from their environment faithfully.

I imagine the mind as a large underground garage housing transport containers. The door of one of the containers says "Money." Inside the money container is all the information you have about the money you have collected so far, and that represents your level of awareness regarding money. All your views, opinions, and experiences are there. To change your income, you must first go to that container where this information is located and replace the ideas that are there that are no longer serving you. This container of money is responsible for producing your monetary reality because your thinking comes from the ideas stored there. Until you change the ideas in this container, your reality about money will not change. It's that simple. The door of this container is called the barrier. It will prevent you from even entering. It will make you feel uncomfortable when you think differently from the thoughts written in it. You need to break through the door and consciously repeat new ideas to plant new money ideas that will serve you better. If you look carefully at your financial life, you will notice that it is followed by one thread, one pattern with minor oscillations. You always have the same amount of money. Sometimes it happens that you earn more than you normally do on an annual basis, but that extra is gone very quickly, so the next year you earn less than usual. That golden thread that has followed you all your life is a pattern of a financial paradigm.

Since childhood we have been programmed to live through our senses. When we look at our earnings, we say it is our condition. It's not our condition. Current earnings are just proof that in the past we were focused on that amount. Most people continue to think the same things, the things they are surrounded by. The outside world controls them that way. Changing any paradigm is not an easy job because internal resistance is big and powerful. That is why it is necessary to repeat new ideas as much as possible every day. In addition to the imagination exercise, through which you spend an abundance of money, you need to take a piece of paper and describe in detail every morning when you wake up how much money you have, how much you earn, and where you invest and spend that money. That piece of paper serves as a new program for your money container. It must be repeated thousands of times, the same way that the first information got there. It is the only way to get out of the vicious circle of your paradigm — by writing a new financial paradigm.

Money is in the consciousness. It's not on the outside. You need to carry the money in your consciousness, just as you now carry the amount you have in your account. All the tools a person needs to live this life are already in him.

Therefore, it is useless to look outside for anything you do not currently have. All it takes is to develop these tools and learn how to get what you want. Your whole life is your own manifested consciousness. Nothing is hidden. The world really is your mirror.

Money can be attracted. If you do not have money, it is proof that you do not have it in your thoughts. You are not aware of it, and you don't have the idea of money planted in you. Someone now has $100,000 in their home, someone who has already become aware of it. Someone else has several million.

There is a Bible quote that says, "He who has will be rewarded, and he who does not have will be deprived even of what he has." What does that mean? It means that the one who has money in his consciousness, who is on the frequency of money, will get more, and the one who does not will be deprived even of what he has. This quote applies to all spheres of life, not just the financial part.

I heard the story of a man who got on a plane to Paris to go shopping. He and his wife had about $20,000 in cash they planned to spend. When the plane landed and passengers were allowed to pack and get off the plane, the man stopped next to his seat. He waited behind the other passengers to get off the plane. At that moment, another man next to him was taking his carry-on luggage from the storage space above his seat, and he pulled a piece of paper out with his luggage, which fell at the feet of the first man, who was watching it. It was money. He picked the money up and asked the gentleman beside him if it was his money, to which he replied that it was not. He looked at the other gentleman in front of him and asked if the money was his, to which he again received the answer that it was not. Then he took that money and put it in his pocket. He later saw that these were two $100 bills. Not only did he have $20,000 with him but the universe sent him another $200 just in case.

Everything works under the same laws. It is our duty to learn these laws and consciously apply them in our lives.

MULTIPLE SOURCES OF INCOME

Making money is a game. Work is the worst way to make money because you will run out of time. No matter the worth of your working hour, you will always be limited to those 60 minutes. The key to financial freedom is to establish multiple sources of income. You can make money while you sleep, so much so that you cannot spend it all when you are awake. The richest people in the world work the least. They understand this game of money. Today, in the age of the Internet revolution, establishing multiple sources of revenue is much easier because communication is almost instantaneous. There's a whole world in front of you and people you can offer something to as your service. But you need to take the time to first think in the direction of establishing different sources of income. Just like in a supermarket, if one product goes out of stock, the business will not stop, because there are plenty of other products that sell and maintain the business, even without the one that is currently gone. It is the same with money. Relying on your own work is the same as when a supermarket sells only one product. It doesn't matter if your one income is $50 a month, another $ 500, and a third $1000. They all have something in common, which is that they merge into one account — your account. All rich people have multiple sources of income. It is time to adopt a new way of thinking, the thinking of rich people. A passive source of income is the best way to get rich. Once you've created passive income streams, you don't have to spend a lot of time maintaining them. They will continue to grow more and more so that you won't even notice that there are streams of money pouring into your account.

EXAMPLES OF GREAT & BAD SERVICES

Money won't come in a bag to your front door just because you're imagining it. The universe will respond to your vibe, giving you opportunities and resources to make money.

It will be necessary to provide a service to make money. There's no such thing as something for nothing. The universe is fair, and in return, you will be given exactly what you provided. If you give your customers bad intentions, this intention wraps up all the products you sell, and you get the same kind of energy back. You may think that this is not true, that some people have money even though they are really bad; however, their money is only a temporary victory. You should be happy when you are providing fair service with honest intention because only then will your customers come to you in huge numbers. We are vibrational beings living in physical bodies. Through the intuitive factor, we can feel the vibrations of other people. When you provide the service and think only of yourself and your needs, you will not succeed in the long run. Your sales will decline because you do not fulfill the purpose of the sale in that case.

Many people fail to see this from the right angle. At a conscious level, the seller seems to be happy to sell a product and help you, but at a subconscious level, the seller hopes that by buying the product, you will actually help him. As vibrational beings, we have the capacity to sense this intention, and it will create chaos in our minds. At the conscious level, we hear one piece of information, and in the subconscious, we feel another intention; this creates confusion for us. No sale can arise out of confusion. As the founder of Walmart said, your real boss is the customer, and he can fire you whenever he wants simply by choosing to shop elsewhere. Only a few are able to understand the importance of the customer. Those who are, are most often those who are successful in their field of business. They don't really have competition. They work for the best interests of their clients and, as a result, generate profits.

There is evidence for this in every corner of the world. You don't have to go beyond your city to see this. Take a look at your local grocery store or your hairdresser. They do not grow their business because they do not understand who their boss is.

I once went to a barber shop that was the first of its kind in my city. He provided the traditional haircut service, but he never understood what the job really should look like. To be a gentleman providing a gentleman's service, you must have a place that embodies this intention, and he did not have one. His shop was deserted and dirty. He did not clean regularly after his customers. The furniture was in poor and worn out condition, as was the rest of the equipment. The vibe of this place was really low. I never went back there.

There are similar service providers who think they are important and the only ones in town, so you need to wait a long time for their service. They make you wait because they pretend to be busy, and for some strange reason, naive people temporarily accept this game because they think they are important if they are in a popular place where waiting is a mandatory thing. The universe gave them opportunities, but they failed to see that their real boss is the customer, and as a result, their clients declined drastically, so they had to change their location. If you want to succeed, never let your customers wait for you, because they are not there for you; you and your business are there for them.

◆◆◆

I once traveled to London with my pregnant wife, and we went from the airport straight to Harrods department store for dinner. We were able to find a table at one of their restaurants and ordered a steak. We asked how long we would have to wait for the steak because we were hungry since we had just arrived in London, to which the waiter said 25 minutes, which is the standard preparation time for the steak. We waited 80 minutes with the occasional promise of the waiters that the order would be ready in the next 5 minutes. After that much waiting, a brilliantly prepared steak arrived. When I asked for the bill, the restaurant manager came up with an apology and said the meal was on the restaurant. I tried to refuse because the food was prepared perfectly after all, and it was expensive even by London standards, but the manager honestly insisted on not charging us. He understood the importance of putting the customer first.

◆◆◆

There is a great restaurant in my town that has been providing outstanding service for a full 35 years, and therefore it is the best restaurant in town. The main motto of the restaurant is to provide great service, and this attitude is reflected in every corner of the restaurant. The owner of this place has spent his entire life traveling the world, gathering experiences as a customer and then implementing customer needs into his restaurant. As a result, his business has flourished. The restaurant staff is like one big family. You don't go to a restaurant just for delicious food. The feeling of a good meal starts as soon as you step into a place. The atmosphere of the place itself, the welcome of the staff, and the quality of the food make a restaurant successful. They listen to every need you might have. In this restaurant, among 30 other waiters, there's one that stands out in particular. He respects people and serves them with dignity. He knows when to talk and what to say. He doesn't talk unnecessarily when he gets familiar with his guests. He is very cultured and has good manners. You feel you are in good hands when he serves you. Sometimes it seems to me that this man has the ability to read minds. Whatever I need, he's there the moment I think about it. He watches his guests well and does everything as if he was invisible. He put his guests first, and he does his job perfectly. He provides a much better service than what he's paid for, and in return, he's paid even more for the service he provides.

If you own a business, you need to understand that you are there for the customer, not the other way around. In the end, the money in your customer's wallet is the same money you will use to pay your staff and bills, put gasoline in your car or put money in your savings, and pay for your house and everything in your entire life.

If you work for a company, you realize that you are not paid by that company but through that company. The company earns revenue through customers, and it's easy to understand that you're actually paid by the people you serve directly or indirectly. There are people who mistakenly think that if someone refuses to buy their product, someone else will buy it instead. If you don't treat every customer as the most important person in your shop or company, you probably won't treat others customers right either. Your company, as a result of your poor service, will eventually lose revenue, and we know that a business without revenue must eventually be shut down.

◆◆◆

I worked in London a few years ago. I would carry advertising material door to door, street by street, block by block. It was a low-paid job but enough to survive. We worked as a team. A colleague would cover one side of the street, and I would cover the other. The goal was to distribute as much material as possible in as little time as possible. When the morning was cold and rainy, I watched to get out of the street as soon as possible. I skipped doors and houses, so I would insert advertising material into every third house.

On the other hand, I would see my colleague walking into each yard leaving the material slowly. I had to wait for him at the end of the street because he was three times slower than I was. At the end of the street, I would ask him, "Why are you doing this? Why are you wasting your time loading materials into every door? We are underpaid anyway. We are not going to make big money from this business." He gave me one of the best explanations I could hear, although at the time, I didn't understand it. He said, "You were paid to do this job. You were paid, and you agreed to it. If you don't work at this job properly, you won't at any. It's not about the money; it's about your work ethic. The way you work, by skipping houses, you are hurting everyone, including yourself. Someone paid for the material to be made.

"Someone is paid to create the material. Someone is paid to distribute it. Someone could buy cheaper goods that are on sale and are being promoted through that material. You're cheating on this whole chain, and you're in it. And thus, in the end, you are fooling yourself without even knowing it. If you do not distribute the material to each door in an area as intended and later throw the material in the container, you are harming everyone.

"You are harming the company that paid to promote their products. You are harming the company that prints this material because if the promotion is not positive, they will eventually lose their jobs. You are harming your employer who hired you to distribute the material. You are hurting potential buyers by making them pay more for the same items as these are not on sale elsewhere. You're hurting yourself by having no one to pay you if the job isn't done right."

I memorized this explanation, although I never applied it in this business. I left because I thought I was worth more, which was not true. My attitude at the time reflected exactly what I was worth, and that's exactly how much I made. Imagine how many people around the world have the same approach as I had — a wrong one.

I didn't provide the service I was paid for. Since I did my job the way I did, I was unsuccessful. That's a cosmic moral in the act, and it is infallible. What you give, you'll get back later. It will level out because this universe is fair. It is the law.

◆ ◆ ◆

After this job, I got a job at a nightclub. My earnings were similar to my previous job, but my earning opportunities were higher. How? It's simple. When I came, it was explained to me that bartenders can fill the bottles up with water, and as much as they fill a bottle up, they can put that much in their pocket. I thought, How easy it is to earn £100 a night? I stayed at this job for three months, and although I made good money, I quit. I could no longer look into the eyes of the people who paid fairly while giving them diluted drinks. At the time, I had been reading a book, *The Science of Getting Rich* by Wallace Wattles for several months, and as a result, there was a struggle between what I was reading and what I was doing. On top of that, I had my colleague's advice in mind: If you don't do this job properly, you won't do any.

That is why you will never be paid more than you are worth. You are temporarily cheating people and the cosmos as well. Now, you can certainly think of someone who you know has more money and you know that he or she earned it in an unfair way. People who do this, sooner or later, end up without money or in prison. Man's morality is changeable because it depends on external factors, but the morality of the cosmos, which is the law of existence, cannot be changed. What you give vibrationally to the world, you'll be given in return from that world, sooner or later.

◆◆◆

In one city I listened to a conversation between taxi drivers: "We're standing here and waiting," one of them was shouting. He was an Alfa Taxi driver.

"We are waiting for the fool that we can charge a lot more and then go home. One ride is enough." And then he said he drove clients from the airport to the city center at a price of $200 the day before, and the ride was otherwise worth $20. But he added that his car broke down the same day, and he had to pay $600 for the repair. He said that if he had not "ripped off" those people the day before, he would not have had enough money to pay for the repair. The man did not understand the purpose of the service. The universe also gave him more than what he was giving. If he hadn't set an unfair price, ten times higher, his car would not have broken down.

I was once in Paris and stopped a cab on the street. A middle-aged Japanese man was driving a very neat and tidy car. He himself was quiet. There was classical music playing in the car. The drive around the streets of Paris was truly pleasant. I gave him a tip as a part of the price for the ride. He understood the service providing principle.

I had a woman who was cleaning my apartment twice a week. At first, she did her job as needed. I recommended her to many of my friends. Over time, she looked to get away with things, work less, and stay longer, thus charging more. After only a month, all my friends sent her away. I kept her on for two years because she was a single mother. Every time she came, I would show her how to clean the space better. I tried to encourage her with higher pay, tips, and gifts. However, she could not understand, because the ideas in her subconscious controlled her behavior. I recognized myself in her from the time I worked in London, only my lesson was never learned by her. She didn't understand this. In the end, she lost her job at my place, which is not so terrible; the terrible thing is that if she does not become aware of her views, she will never earn more than she is worth.

◆◆◆

There are many examples of great service that can help us understand what kind of service they provide.

If you go to the Four Seasons Hotel in Paris, you will understand why they are successful. The vibe of that place is amazing. Rarely will you feel such harmony extending through a space. We came to the bar one morning and ordered a drink. My wife wanted fresh orange juice. The waiter asked her if she wanted fresh juice that had been squeezed early in the morning (three hours before we arrived) or if we had time to wait for them to prepare it now. After my wife asked for the freshly squeezed juice, the waiter brought a bottle of water, which normally costs 6 euros, for free so we could refresh ourselves while waiting for the juice. It is an example of providing excellent service. The sacred rule when it comes to work is, the more you provide sincere intentions and services, the more you will be rewarded from the universe in the form of work. This is also true of all other areas of life. You cannot get negative results for positive actions.

If you have a quality product and you provide excep-tional service with it, you will never lose your job. There will be people who will understand your true intentions and philosophy of creation and will always be willing to pay, no matter the cost.

10% IS YOURS TO KEEP

If you want to achieve financial freedom, this is rule number one. Save at least 10% of every dollar you earn. Pay yourself first.

Most people work hard all their lives, but they never learn to pay themselves first. They worked hard but gave it to everyone else. A man pays for gasoline, pays for groceries, and pays for bills but doesn't pay himself. It is his money, but he handed it over to others; that is why he often ends up with no money. Ten percent is the minimum amount that should be left when you make money. It's yours to keep, but the money is not meant to be shut up in a safe. Money is energy whose natural state is to flow. The ten percent that is to be deducted from any profit should be placed on the market when the opportunity arises. When you get a profit from a business opportunity, 10% should be returned and another 10% should be added. This is the key to financial freedom. How many times have you had the opportunity to invest, but you did not have the funds, nor did you have anyone to lend you the money to invest, and that opportunity passed you by?

It happened because you didn't have your own budget for financial freedom.

The truth is that opportunities are always there for whoever can see them. Opportunities are always there, and they are in the eye of the beholder. Even if you are in debt, you need to save 10% of everything you earn. This will help you pay off your debt sooner. When you read this advice for the first time, you may not think your income is sufficient for your basic needs, let alone for setting aside 10%. Ten percent may be relatively low compared to what you are currently earning, but it is not about the amount. It's a habit you develop. This is how you become a magnet for money. You then accumulate energy from the universe because you saved money. You become a banker of the universe. The energy goes where it already is. So an increasing amount will come to you, and you will start seeing more and more opportunities that have always been there but you have not been able to see. This is how you become worthy of the money you desire so much.

PRINCIPLE 4:
Change Your Paradigm by Changing One Habit at a Time

There's something that controls you. That something has the features of a living being. It is paradigm.

A paradigm is a group of habits that has control your behavior and life. It is a mental program that is formed in childhood. Your whole life is a reflection of multiple paradigms because your paradigm influences your perception, influences how you use your time, influences the amount of money you earn, and influences your effectiveness, logic, and creativity.

Paradigms are the mental patterns you get from your authorities. They are passed on from one generation to the next. They are stored in the subconscious and directly affect the vibration your body is in. The action you take must be consistent with the ideas from the subconscious, with paradigms.

Our paradigm controls the way we brush our teeth, the way we walk, how we talk, and how we greet people. It controls the amount of money we make, our health, our appearance, and our friendships. Therefore, it is fair to say that the way we live today is an absolute product of other people's mindsets. Every external stimulus that comes to us before we define its meaning goes through censorship, and the paradigm processes the information and tells us how we will see it. We almost never see things as they are, but we see a distorted picture of each event because the paradigm affects the perception. What is our view regarding wealth, or making money, or friends? These are not even our views; these views are the thinking patterns of the people who raised us. They are responsible for the paradigms that have been formed in us. We have inherited our views and have never questioned them.

When we come up with a new idea through thought, it encounters resistance to the ruling paradigm. These resistances are justifications, and they are always the same ones. The paradigm does not even bother to invent new reasons. The paradigm has various techniques of defending its existence and power in the human subconscious. At first it defends itself with a quiet voice and excuses like these: "Stay in bed another minute. It's Sunday," "Eat that cake; you won't gain weight if you eat one piece of cake," or "Spend that money. You'll earn some more." If you have firmly made the decision to persevere, then the real paradigm awakens. It is like a beast, and it will try its best to stay alive because that is its nature — to survive. It will create various distractions for you, all the way to physical ailments, such as allergies, colds, or serious illnesses. Changing one habit requires a lot of effort and willpower, but changing a group of habits is a war in the subconscious. That is why we have seen countless times, both personally and among the people we know, how people go on a diet, but after three months, they are back to their old habits. And they do it again every year. I recently heard a story from a friend, who is a fitness instructor. He helped his client lose 40 pounds in a few months. I asked him how this man was doing today, and he said, "He is heavier now than he was. He has gained another 70 pounds." It's a paradigm in action. It is struggling to make up for what it has lost.

One may have the paradigm that he often catches a cold at the same time every year. As the weather gets colder, the symptoms of cold and flu begin to manifest, every year without exception. It has nothing to do with viruses or the flu; it's a paradigm in action. A paradigm is a mental program from your subconscious, and it works perfectly. Due to the paradigm, the poor become poorer and the rich become richer. It's not about marketing, and it's not about economics; it's about your programming from the subconscious. The paradigm absolutely controls you.

◆◆◆

Your selling rate and your income are the result of a paradigm. Children's grades at school are the result of a paradigm as well. Your health is the result of a paradigm. Your social and love life are the reflection of a paradigm. It all starts from a habit that joins with other habits to create a paradigm, and various paradigms, when joined, create a reflection of your life and current achievements. The good news is that paradigms can be changed.

HOW TO DISCOVER A PARADIGM

Write your goal on a piece of paper — something you'd like to achieve but don't see how it could be done at this time. After a few moments, your first thoughts and justifications of why you can't do it will start appearing. It is a paradigm quietly whispering the thoughts over and over. These are thoughts that have been repeated so many times in your mind that you now firmly defend them because you think they are yours. The paradigm defends itself at first with justifications and then goes silent for a while. It is waiting for an auspicious opportunity to express itself. It is a mental program from the subconscious, and it knows your subconscious better than you do yourself. Scientists have come to the conclusion that it takes 21 days to form a new habit. A paradigm is a group of habits and is much more powerful. It is ready to not show itself for 90 days if you persist in changing one or two habits at a time. It will wait patiently, and you will think you beat it. And then you will be at a party and someone will offer you one small piece of cake. That's no big deal; you've been persistent for 90 days. You are no longer a sugar addict, you have improved your weight, and you look better, so it's time to treat yourself to a mouthful of sweet cake. That one cake is your paradigm in action. It is subtle, wise, and persevering, and it knows the terrain better than you do. It knows the neural networks that are tied to your emotions and memory. It knows your trigger mechanisms for its activation. It knows your character. It has the features of a living being, and for its own conservation, it will fight till the very end, using whatever is available to it — from the voice that arrives through thoughts to rational and irrational fears, worry, and anxiety, all the way to real illness.

The subconscious is a part of the old primitive consciousness people were created with. It is big and powerful, and it houses all the emotions, which are very fast. They are fast like animals: They have extraordinary reflexes, react lightly, and cannot be controlled. Because of this, the person is quickly annoyed and quick to react, and only after those animals return to their cages does he wonder what was wrong with him. Consciousness is the tip of the iceberg, and below it there is an invisible animal kingdom that is over-whelming, powerful, and strong.

Collective paradigms can be seen in nations, or in one nation located in different regions within a state. If it's been ten years since you left your hometown, when you come to visit, you'll notice that your peers have remained frozen in time. They continued to preserve the tradition without even noticing that they were preserving it. Their speech, appearance, behavior, and beliefs are the image of one collective paradigm of that city.

HOW TO CHANGE A PARADIGM

There are two ways to change a paradigm. One is emotional shock, when something shakes you so much that it literally breaks the roots of the paradigm. Another way is to constantly repeat the new idea. Whenever you want to change the paradigm, start with one habit. Never change multiple habits at once, because the paradigm is very powerful.

If you change five habits a year and continue for the next five years, you will change 25 key habits, which will change you as a person at the cellular level.

It is imperative that you be persistent and disciplined. Even the current paradigms that control your social, financial, or emotional life have not emerged in 21 days. They were nurtured for a long period of time, regularly, every day. An idea was repeated to you thousands of times before it got its fortification in your subconscious. The paradigm changes the same way: by repeating one idea countless times. Old paradigms almost never die. Their power over you begins to weaken when you stop giving them attention, but they are always on standby, patiently waiting for the moment of your weakness to reappear. It will wait for years, and it will always try to wake up again through the silent voice in your head. If you give up once and stay in bed longer, the paradigm gains power. It will soon reappear as a thought in your head and, at the first opportunity, will invite you to stay longer in bed the next morning. It will also give you a symptoms of a cold so you do not feel well and thus have a realistic justification for staying in bed.

The paradigm uses the excuse that something is real, and it only seems realistic to us. Realistic is never realistic. In the word itself, the real is the king, and the king commands. We give what seems realistic to us the right to command the situation. To something that by its very nature is unpainted and neutral, we give the right to be realistic and central. The reality is, what you are reading is distorted by your paradigm. That's why each of you will interpret the lines you read differently.

◆◆◆

Paradigms change gradually and with innumerable repetitions. You can write down your perfect life or the main habit that you want to change. It is necessary to do the imagining every day because it is one of the main ways to change the paradigm. Every time you see a scene in your mind and feel excited, you become stronger than the current paradigm.

◆◆◆

Imagine wanting to conquer a fortress that has existed in one place for several decades. You came to a nearby grove with a few of your friends during the night. These fellows are called will, imagination, reason, thinking, and persistence. Your friends are out of shape and have not had a decent amount of training for a long time but have agreed to follow the path under your command. Will you run with them straight to the main gate of that fort? Do you know that the guards from the fortress were expecting you even before you reached that grove? They are informed of your intentions and plans; they are ready and expecting you. The messengers are already arranged along the walls of the fortress, silently repeating the same thoughts to distract you from your intention even before you've arrived.

To conquer a fortress, you need to infiltrate and conquer it from the inside, section by section, and not be noticed. That's why you've read that when you want to change your life, the change must not be forced. Just as the water flows effortlessly, that's how you should change the old conditioning.

Until the paradigm changes, nothing changes. It provides security. Your life may not be too exciting, but it is comfortable. What most do not know is that if the paradigm does not change, life will gradually degrade in all fields as energy is always moving. Nothing stands still. You either grow in consciousness or you recede.

PRINCIPLE 5:
Focus Only on What You
Want to See in Your Life

Everything that happens every moment is, by its nature, neither good nor bad. It just is. We, as observers, color the events as good or bad.

It is very easy to see the negative in a situation or a person. Anyone can do that. But to see the good in something that looks bad requires awareness. It is a habit that every person who strives to develop their personality should develop. The law of polarity says that when there is a problem, there is opportunity. The bigger the problem, the greater the opportunity. How many times have you gone on the road and there are simply some things that are stopping you from going. You are on your way, and you have to return home to retrieve the bag you forgot. You are in a hurry to get there, but the car just breaks down on the road and puts off all your plans. Or someone obstructs your movements in traffic, and you have no opportunity to bypass it.

All these things happen for a reason and happen for your own good. You can get nervous about it, thinking that circumstances are hindering you, but in fact, I believe they are happening for your own good. Therefore, these interferences should be viewed as a positive experience. Instead of getting nervous, be happy and just observe. Instead of being upset that it isn't working out as planned, stop and pay attention to the good behind it. There is good and bad in everything, and it is up to you to choose what you will see in it. It all depends on perception. What you focus on will grow in your life because you are giving it energy. If you are upset about traffic jams, you give that vibe to the cosmos and get more traffic jams in your life — maybe not in traffic but in the line at the bank later that day. Train yourself to be patient in these situations. Patience is not the ability to wait; patience is the ability to remain calm while you wait.

Getting fired from your job isn't necessarily a bad thing. You've simply been made redundant. You no longer have that job. Just accept it. The universe helps you in this way as well because you might not have quit on your own. How will you get a better job if you don't leave the old job? If you do not end the toxic relationship you are in, how will you attract the right person for you? If the person you think you love leaves you, don't look at it as something bad. Observe that there is a huge opportunity ahead of you because you are now in a position to attract the person you have wanted for so long.

Everything just is. It is an attitude that leads us to prosperity. Then you flow like a river or a stream, with no resistance. Indulge yourself in the circumstances of your life. Take that extra step in each area, and let things happen on their own. You can only get annoyed by them because you do not see the bigger picture, nor do you have the knowledge and resources necessary to accomplish what you want in your life.

We tend to limit the manifestation of life. Life is abundantly expressed in all areas because everything comes from and everything returns to an infinite center that is equally present all around us each moment.

People often want something to happen to them in a certain way. When they remember their desires, after a while, the momentum they have already given to that aspiration begins to be reflected in their lives. But often people continue to focus on other things and forget their aspirations. When they finally appear in a different form, they resent and blame everything on the outside. They blame fate, children, parents, or friends and forget that they are the source of the condition they see now.

People get a medical diagnosis from a doctor that may not necessarily be correct, and what do they do then? They begin to focus their attention on that diagnosis. They begin to tell friends and relatives what they have been told, take the role of the victim, and think that they are not being treated fairly by life. After a while, they really start to feel bad. They persuade their subconscious mind to have the disease they were told, even though they do not have it. The subconscious, however, receives all emotional ideas as real, and it, in relation to the cosmic power, begins to give symptoms to the body. They really do get sick. There are a number of problems that people pose to themselves because they have focused on the wrong news that came from the outside. They are not in control of their lives. Circumstances control them.

The only energy your brain cells can receive is the energy they give. If you focus on the negative in people or situations, what do you think the energy you draw will be? How do you think you will vibrate? We are conditioned to see only what already exists in us. The next time you are angry with someone, know that this energy must flow through you the moment you send it. And at that very moment, you programmed your brain cells to receive only that kind of energy.

A story about an American World War II soldier, Desmond Thomas Doss, holds the evidence of this cosmic law. He refused to carry a weapon during the war and instead served as a paramedic in the war to help his fellow soldiers. Doss refused to kill any man and therefore could not be killed!

Although he was wounded four times in the famous Battle of Okinawa, he managed to rescue as many as 75 of his comrades, for which he received the Medal of Honor in 1945. He was unable to receive the energy he was not prepared to give. Although wounded, he remained alive and received great respect from the combatants as well as his people. What a great lesson to be drawn from his example. Do not condemn so you wouldn't be condemned. Don't cheat so you won't be cheated. Refuse to do harm, and harm won't find its way to you. That's the law of existence.

As already mentioned, everything comes from subtle dimensions to the physical dimension we live in. We contact the higher dimensions with the help of the mind and its qualities. The properties of the conscious part of the mind are reason, will, imagination, perception, memory, and intuition. Where do people get it wrong? They look at what there is, and they create more of it. Nothing changes. We use memory to remember how much money we have in our account and create more. The force that flows into us every moment has no form. It just is.

We have the ability to imagine whatever we want. When we transpose this idea we imagine into the subconscious, it is only a matter of time before it will emerge in our world. It is a creative process and it is at our disposal, but we are using it wrongly because instead of using our imagination and imagining a new amount in our bank account, we look at what there is, or what there was last month, and so we repeat the results. If you want to make more money this month than you did last month, use your imagination and imagine that you already have what you want. You must not allow what you see to control your emotions, because your emotions adjust the vibration of your body, which must take action relative to the vibration it is in. If you allow your emotions to be driven by results, know that nothing new will happen. So you run the risk of an even lower vibration and worse results.

What should we do when we have bills to pay and we don't have money? We have the ability to choose how we feel about that situation. If we consciously apply these laws of life, we can accept that we have to pay our bills and feel good about it. Why would we feel bad if we didn't have the money to pay the bills? Bad feelings put us in a bad vibe, and we can't create anything positive out of that bad vibe. Our point of attraction is now. If we can't pay our bills now, we can still feel good about ourselves. From a positive vibe, we can think of a way to handle this situation. If you are already in a situation where you cannot meet your obligations, know that this is not the first time. That situation came back into your life because in the past, you felt bad about a similar situation and you created that same situation. It doesn't mean we should ignore our obligations, but we can stay in control of our thoughts, feelings, and vibrations and figure out a way to pay the bills, even if we don't see it clearly at first.

It's called thinking. How do most people work? They do not think but react. The only difference between us and animals is that we have the capacity to think. We often do not think but rather respond to external stimulation. The cause of all the misfortune in people's lives is non-thinking. They react instead of thinking and thus find themselves in a vicious circle of negative vibrations, which manifest themselves as situations they have no control over.

Over a hundred years ago, Wallace Wattles wrote in his book, *The Science of Getting Rich*:

To think health when surrounded by the appearances of disease, or to think riches when in the midst of appearances of poverty, requires power; but he who acquires this power becomes a MASTER MIND. He can conquer fate; he can have whatever he wants.

Unsuccessful people respond to what is happening to them completely unaware that they and their feelings are the cause of those events. Successful people know that they are the cause of the event, and when something happens that they did not anticipate, they don't get nervous. They remain calm and seek a solution. They do not panic or let fear control them. Everyone can be successful if they learn to think. You can believe that something else is the cause, you can blame other people for your results, and you can believe that the events came by chance, but if you look at yourself and your results, you will notice that they are always a mirror of your deepest beliefs and attitudes. Your world is a reflection of your thought patterns.

◆◆◆

Every situation is temporary, and it is up to you to decide whether to extend it or to terminate it. The poor mind cannot create wealth, because the poor mind does not see wealth. It is restrained by its limitations because it is focused on the disadvantages. What about what we thought before? The moment we start working in a new light, that shift begins.

Just like when we start taking a new therapy, for the first couple of days, there is no sign of anything changing, but after a while, the first signs of change occur. What is important to keep in mind is that in moments of change, situations that have to do with the past will surely occur as this is just one of the old paradigm's attempts to bring us back through old fear, old thinking, and old behaviors. It's a normal part of the game. We have to go ahead with the new plan, and the old conditioning will weaken due to lack of attention.

If we keep finding ourselves in the same situations, it is because we do not understand or accept them. We did not understand that they happened because of us, to help us become aware of something in us. All uncomfortable situations we are stuck in, and when we suffer, have a common trait, which is us blaming something or someone on the outside. We do not accept our role and responsibility and that it happened because of us. The moment we accept this, however, things start to change. These patterns stop being maintained and repeated. Then we move on to a higher level of experience. We thus get new situations whose purpose is the same: to raise our level of awareness. Everything happens because of us. It teaches us to become more aware. Having a bad employer gives you the opportunity to learn how to be a better employer. If you have gone bankrupt, it teaches you how to manage your money properly. If you have a bad relationship, it teaches you how to be better at relationships. Every situation carries an opportunity where you can learn something.

The more aware and alert you are, the less you will condemn those people you do not like. Someone else's unawareness acts as a mirror, affecting us just as much as we are unaware and thus helping us to become aware. All relationships between people are based on different levels of awareness or maturity. All that people argue about is essentially a misunderstanding of someone else's level of awareness. All they agree on is their understanding of the state of awareness of the other. Usually the ones that annoy you the most have the most important role to play. Their role is to bring to light what you are unaware of and what you need to experience for some reason and yet refuse to do it. That's why they make you uncomfortable. Anything that is unpleasant is actually what you need to become aware of in yourself, by so you don't see it but rather are projecting the inconvenience on those who bring it out. These are often emotional things that must be lived with and worked on and not just communicated and mentally understood.

◆ ◆ ◆

Always take notice of how you feel in the present moment. Your whole life is woven from the present moment, and your point of creation is always now. You always create now, and what you are looking at now invites the same things to come tomorrow, that is, to the new now. Whenever you have an unpleasant situation, do not mindlessly react to it but respond meaningfully. Try to be aware that your point of creation is always in the present moment and that what you see comes from the past point of some present moment. If you are recounting past events in the present moment, you are inviting experiences that have the same or similar vibration. They do not appear exactly the same and in the same place, but they have a common intensity. If you are dreaming of beautiful things in the present moment, you are inviting experiences that are beautiful. If you are now afraid that you will not have enough money to survive this month, and if you worry about it for a few days, you have created a similar experience for some future present moment that will come to you. You may not find the cause between today's worries and not having money for months, but they are in a cause and effect relationship. That is why we are said to be co-creators. We are literally creating our subjective reality within objective reality through how we feel about every present moment. Bearing in mind that we are beings who change their moods very quickly, it is not at all unusual that we are healthy today and sick tomorrow, rich then poor. On a microplane, we unconsciously follow the macro cosmic laws of rhythm because everything changes. In short, do not look into your bank account or the previous month to decide how you should feel. Although today may not be the way you want it to be, you can always change the future.

If you are aware that what you see now came from what you looked at yesterday, then you know that what you are looking at now decides what you will see tomorrow.

◆ ◆ ◆

You become what you think.

Let's explain what this means so everyone can truly understand. You become what you think. By this, I do not mean the thoughts that your mind has picked up from the ether thrown out by other minds as cosmic waves. Here we think of thoughts that are deeply embedded in your subconscious mind as deep beliefs and ideas, where your thinking comes from. Who implanted these ideas in you? Your educators and your environment when you were a child. Before the age of five, your subconscious is open, and everything that surrounds you is flowing into it. Your critical thinking skills are not developed, so children do not have the ability to consciously reject any idea that is repeated to them over and over. The problem arises after the age of five, when you begin to express these ideas through behavior as your own, and then they become even deeper and stronger as habits are created. The habits you protect, though, aren't yours. Millions of people around the world are suffering throughout their lives, trying to get rid of the chains of slavery chains of someone else's habits that were instilled in them when they were children. If you don't have a central idea leading you through your life, you will become the tool of the state, religion, or educational system. If, on the other hand, you have a strong desire to change your life, no conditioning can hold you back. You become what you want to be with your whole being. Nature always finds a way to manifest itself.

You will not experience something until you start believing it is possible.

This is why it is so critical to acquire faith before you attempt to achieve any goal. If you do not have faith, you will miss the target even when your target is close. In fact, even if your target is close to you, you can't perceive it until you start having faith. The target does not yet exist for you.

An important thing to remember is that you do not need to have previous experience in order to believe. Your belief can be based on a lie or on another person's success story you have heard. But once it is formed, your belief will always tend to produce experience for you as a fact.

This is the magical law of the universe.

Money, pain, lack, or misfortune do not exist until you call them into focus.

PRINCIPLE 6:
Thinking, the Greatest
Human Virtue

There is a difference between true thinking and the everyday thoughts that go through our heads. Thoughts are cosmic waves. They enter our minds, mix with the content that exists there, and form thoughts that most people misinterpret as thinking. That's not thinking at all. It's a mental activity. Thinking, by contrast, is a creative process. Only a few people think. The others do not think and are not aware of it at all. Most people are like a cork in the ocean carried by the waves. If people would think, they would never say or do most of the things they say and do. All the actions they take come from the subconscious in response to an external stimulus. Thus a person is put into the same state of consciousness that animals have.

It may sound harsh, but it is so. Look around you. People don't think. We have various thoughts throughout our day that go through our minds like a cloud. Most often they do not have potential because they do not have momentum. It is not thinking but the mind's way of dealing with the associative concepts that it notices through the senses. We see one situation, and our mind quickly looks at the notions from our memory, which are connected by experience with what we see and give us, like a librarian, a file about it; then we begin to talk about it. This is an automatic operation of the mind and a habit. It is not thinking, and it does not have the power of creation.

Take a city walk for example. We see a window decorated with New Year's Eve decorations, and our minds quickly find a notion in our memory that is consistent with these ornaments and begins an internal monologue. If we are with someone else, we start uncontrollably talking about what we see in our minds. It often happens that within just one minute, the mind jumps from story to story without it being noticed by us or our companion.

Why are you going to work? A job is the worst way to earn money. In the age of the Internet revolution, where information is available with a simple click, there is no excuse for a person to remain poor. Today anyone can become financially independent if they start thinking. As children, we learned not to think. We were conditioned to react rather than respond to external events. When we react, we do not think. When we react, we are not in control of our lives. Only when we stop our emotional reaction do we begin to think. We are conditioned to do what others do and to never ask why we do it.

People are the only beings on the planet who have the ability to think. The average person thinks several times during the year, most often when a disaster strikes him. Only then does the person temporarily stop the impulsive reaction to events and begin to think creatively about the problem that has hit him. In other cases, one does not think but repeats patterns of behavior in response to what surrounds him. That is why it is said that a person is asleep. People can only grow in knowledge, consciousness, and life if they use the natural capacity of the mind and the ability to think. Only then does one live; everything else is superficial survival. That's why Descartes said, "I think there I am." When a man really thinks, then he is. He is present in every situation. He is not a cork that the sea throws where it wants but is the captain of his vessel, which moves like an albatross to meet the storm.

One has to find within him the hidden reasons why he behaves the way he does and examine them critically. Most people have created behavior patterns by mimicking authority even when they were young. Pay attention to yourself and to the people around you. They walk, dress, talk, look, and act like their parents. They don't think, and they almost don't exist.

They are a faithful replica of their environment. The worst part about this is that they are not even aware of it. They are not aware that their lives are not theirs. Without question, they became the perpetrators of other's habits. Some of these habits were established several generations before and have never been questioned. If our ancestors, for lack of information and limited technology, had to act a certain way 100 years ago, why are we blindly following their examples? We have information available all around us. We can start thinking. We can transform a formless substance that flows into our mind into any form. We have the ability to do this. We have the will, and we have the imagination. We can create whatever we want. We do not have to abide by the old limiting beliefs of our authorities. We can live the life we want and are destined for in peace, in abundance, and in happiness.

◆◆◆

Many people have ruined their lives by reacting to what is happening to them and have been left to repent all of their lives due to a few moments of not thinking. We have the ability to stop the reaction and think of a way to respond to any situation.

How many times have you run into trouble yourself while in traffic because in your opinion, someone is not acting right and getting in your way. You do not have to react. You can always stop your emotions and use reason to respond to the situation as best as you can. You certainly will not teach anyone anything if you scold or physically attack him or her. In fact, the reason why he or she behaves in a way that annoys you is the same reason you act that way, which is not thinking.

Whatever happened in your life, you have the choice to respond rather than react. It is a virtue possessed by human beings and one of the greatest virtues by which we stand out from the animal world. When you start thinking, whether it is the current traffic situation or whether it is the loss of a job or a loved one, or maybe bad news about your health, then you are lifting your life to the heights where one becomes human. Then you become the captain of your life, and you decide where to go next because you are the decision maker.

PRINCIPLE 7:
Be Grateful
for the Small Things

Gratitude is one of the qualities that brings you into harmony with the universe. Gratitude is a confirmation that you have what you are looking for. It is a process of sending vibrations of a positive nature that are harmonious and creative. Most people are only thankful in situations where they get something from someone, and some are not thankful even then. Many of us act as if everything belongs to them, and they take it for granted. How often do you take your body for granted? Your body is the perfect vehicle to move in this dimension of existence. Without it, life is not possible. But the majority of us take it for granted, and we do not pay attention to the basic needs of our bodies. We know very little about how our bodies function. They faithfully serve us, executing our conscious commands while performing automatic functions. How grateful are you to be able to see, hear, and walk? We allow ourselves to overeat and put the wrong foods in our bodies. We live with the rapid development of technologies that allow us to more easily communicate, move around, and perform a handful of actions without any hassle. Despite this, according to available data, as many as 600 million people in India do not have a toilet. Can you imagine your day without the privacy of your toilet?

There are many examples of where we take life for granted without a moment of gratitude while at the same time complaining that we have no money or that our life is not as we would like it to be. When we begin to appreciate what we have in the present moment, then everything starts to change for the better. Acceptance is a harmonious vibration without resistance. The source that all things come from is inexhaustible and responds to our vibrations at every present moment. Nobody owes you anything. If you would look from the point of existence itself, we are the ones who owe the very nature of existence for our existence. But we accepted everything we were given for free and forgot about that debt. Then we turned to our outside world and started blaming everything on the outside if we didn't get it right. Someone said that charity is carved into sand and crime into stone. The great cosmic effort that is put into creating us is carved into the sand, and tiny human unconscious mistakes are being carved into stone every day. It is time to change the perception through which we look at life.

It is time to start appreciating when we see a bird in the air, smell the flowers in the meadow, and catch the smile of a young child. It is time to focus on what we want to see in our lives. It's time to stop gossiping about our brothers and sisters, our acquaintances and friends, and it's time to stop complaining about all those things that bother us. It is time for us to become adults through understanding — adults who responsibly accept their consequences and understand that we are the only ones who have produced these results in our lives. When we truly do all of this and begin to apply it as part of our daily habits, it won't be long before we see endless answers in every form from the center of the universe.

Being grateful means being in a state of peace. Through gratitude, we begin to be present more and more in the here and now, raising the level of vibration of our being and aligning ourselves with life itself and the source of everything that exists. Then, when we feel that we need nothing more, we become a candidate for abundance. When you are happy about what you have, even if it is not enough in comparison to your expectations, your message that you send to the center of the existence of all things is of a positive nature, and it is a signal to the center to send abundance toward you.

PRINCIPLE 8:
Forgive Yourself First

Forgiveness is one of the healthiest concepts we can learn. When we forgive, we release everything that bothers us. We know that every disease first arises at an energy level, and after a certain continuous irritation, that disease overflows into our bodies and produces various disorders. Many people became ill because they could not forgive. Forgiveness has nothing to do with the other person. Forgiveness only has to do with you. When you forgive the other person, you are actually forgiving yourself. You are doing good to your being then and will feel better. It doesn't matter what someone else did to you. Release all these thoughts and move on with your life. Do you know that you're not really bothered by another person but by an idea? The person who did something wrong to you may have long since departed from this world, and you still have negative feelings about that person who no longer exists, which makes you feel bad. Holding on to negative feelings about someone or something that has already happened will only pass through you and thus only harm you.

The energy you hold against someone is yours. It affects you as long as you hold it. Therefore, forgiveness is a healthy concept.

Forgiveness has nothing to do with anyone else. When you forgive, you release your being from these negative vibrations and allow yourself to breathe free again. This is achieved by understanding. That's why Solomon said, " "And with all thy getting get understanding."

That's the key. Maybe someone did something wrong to you, but there is nothing more you can do about it. You cannot change what happened. It stands for eternity. Being angry with someone means taking on the role of victim and rejecting responsibility for what happened. If you hadn't felt how you felt first, you would have never experienced what you experienced.

With this understanding of life and how the universe works, you can understand that the one who does the wrong and the one who receives it, in a sense, share a common responsibility. The results you are seeing are yours alone. You may not like them, but you don't have to look far to see how you got them. That is why in The Alchemist, the treasure was always in the same place where the traveler started the journey. He didn't have to tour half the world to find it. The answer was in him, in the subconscious. In your subconscious, where innumerable fears and imaginary problems lie, the cosmic philharmonic plays and invokes the existence of events that can hear the melody. That is why, according to the hoponopono principle, we thank the one who has done us wrong for having to bear the great sacrifice for our sake. I deeply believe that all the things we have experienced and survived have brought with them the semenases development of our being.

In the conscious and unconscious package, we have two parts. One is the front, like a shop window, and the other is a warehouse where we dump all the garbage. We ourselves don't want to know what's in our warehouse nor do we want to look inside. That's where everything we don't like comes from. And even if we don't like it, we take some of it, look at our world around us, and consider who we would throw it at and say, "It's his or hers and not mine." When we hear someone say, "He rude," "She is rude," or "Look how he or she behaves," it is as if he or she is saying you are rude. If you bring awareness to your behavior, you will notice that the whole world is your mirror of your attitudes and actions. Everything happens because of us. This life is a great school, and every act and misdeed we provide and receive is nothing more than a lesson in developing our own and other's consciousness.

When you hate someone, you become hate at the cellular level because the hate process is inside of you. Hatred and guilt are the worst human emotions. One is directed against the other and the other is directed against yourself, but you are the one who gets both because both emotions are in you. That's why, over time, people who hate other people become just like those people they hate. It doesn't matter if someone did something to you; you will get what you sow. Let the universe take care of those who have done wrong. You can have peace because the universe is just. Justice does not necessarily come from one who has experienced injustice.

FIND YOUR LIFE
BY DISCOVERING
YOUR PURPOSE

I believe that we are not born by accident or that our lives are the result of chance. We are born with a specific purpose. Unfortunately, the vast majority of people on the planet are unaware of this and have turned their lives into safe steps, without a purpose or goals.

Why were we born? We were not born to work from 9 to 5 at a job we do not like, to go to a few celebrations, then retire and step toward death. There must be a better reason why we're here. The purpose of life is life itself, but people have another purpose they live for, even if they're not aware of it. We are spiritual beings who have decided to descend to this plane of existence and in this form. There is a central purpose in each of us, which is the answer to the question of why we were born.

Unless you discover your purpose, your life will never be fulfilled. You can be completely healthy and have all the money in the world, but if you are not aware of your true purpose, you will quietly suffer; your being will be aware that something is missing, deep inside.

How do we know if we are living a life that has purpose and meaning? Simply ask yourself if you are happy with how you spend your days.

If you are not, then you are not living your purpose. To be happy, you have to do what you love. Then you will get up with a smile, looking forward to the day ahead. In the evening, you will lie down with the joy of wanting to get up as soon as possible and once again spending your days filled with deep purpose.

There's a wonderful story about an American billionaire, Kenneth Behring. He revealed his purpose in the later years of his life. He had a wonderful family and lots of money and possessions, but he wasn't happy. Everything he would buy for himself would only be a passing pleasure. He had a yacht, cars, and a big house, but he wasn't happy. Then he thought that if he bought a bigger yacht and a bigger house, he would be happy at last. Again, it was only instant gratification. Then he thought he would find happiness if he bought a football team. That didn't fulfill him either. He simply felt that the life he lived was not in harmony with his being. He was missing something, and he couldn't figure out what it was. Then one day, a friend called him and asked him to go to Bosnia with him to distribute wheelchairs to children who had lost their extremities in the war. As he was handing the wheelchairs to those children, one boy told him that he wanted to look at him again and remember his face so that when he died, he could thank him again in heaven for helping him. Then Kenneth started crying uncontrollably; those tears on his face were not an expression of sadness but happiness. It was then that he realized his purpose: to help children around the world. Following this, he created his foundation and has since distributed hundreds of thousands of wheelchairs around the world. In his book, he advises us not to wait till we are old to discover our purpose.

Every morning when you get up, sit in a quiet place and think about what you like to do the most. Contemplate this idea. It can take weeks, maybe even months, until you get the right answer, but the answer you will receive will be felt throughout your whole being. It doesn't have to be the current job you do. It doesn't even have to be a paid job. You may think that you are devoting all your free time to family and an income-generating job and do not have enough time to do anything else. Regardless, you still must ask yourself what you like to do most. When you discover the right answer, you will find time for it. At first, you may not be making money from that job, but as time goes by, you can think of how what you love to do can give you enough income to leave the job you currently work but do not love.

This is your life. As far as we know, it is the only one. Spend it in happiness and joy, filled with hours you will no longer count or wait to pass. When you discover your purpose, the hours and days will become short because you'll be doing what you love.

◆ ◆ ◆

You don't know who you are, where you are, or why you are. You assume that you are living one life on Earth. But you don't know what it means to be human nor do you know what this planet is or what this life itself is. You are much more than you think you are; you just don't know it yet. You are all that you observe. You are the very intelligence that exists and is. This is why thoughts become things and experiences. A thought doesn't become a thing because one person can do it and another can't. Every human being can do it because every human being is the eternal offshoot of pure consciousness, which is the basis of existence. Consciousness in you is what invokes the existence of every thought so you can have whatever you want, be whatever you want, and live as you wish. You just have to see it first in your mind. You must breathe life to every thought in the workshop of your mind. Your imagination is a life-creating workshop. There is nothing new in this factory. This factory is the last link in creation. It is merely a stage for what has already been created . How could anything new originate in the factory, if it did not first exist in someone's mind?

You live in the world of manifested ideas.

◆ ◆ ◆

Your clock is ticking. None of us know how much time we have left. You may think you will live another 50–60 years, but the reality is likely different. According to unofficial data, about 150,000 people leave this planet every day who thought they would live a long life just the day before.

Do you know that the most valuable currency in the universe is time, not money? When your time is up, the game is over — and with it, all of your dreams, unlived experiences, unseen lands, and unspoken loves are over as well. And the most important thing to understand is that the game does not end at the same time for everyone. The end of the game has nothing to do with your age and comes unannounced. You don't know how many more breaths you have. Maybe it's time to start living your life with more meaning.

Time is the eternal line of the present that goes back to infinity. Our bodies age because matter moves. We perceive matter movement as a flow of time, although it is not. Every day we are one day closer to death. Many people are not aware of this and waste their time on doing the same thing over and over. You may think something is just going to change without you doing anything about your life. I know a lot of people who believe this wrong idea and are noticeably a year older every Christmas and not a penny richer. They continue to maintain the same thinking, which keeps them trapped in the same place for a long period of time.

The good news is that every day your life begins anew. It is new and unwritten. You can do whatever you want if you stop being a slave to yesterday's habits. This requires awareness, willpower, perseverance, and discipline.

By your birth in this body, it has been planned for you to be more than a signature in the water.

Nothing physical or intellectual can give you freedom. You are free once you realize that your bondage arises from your own actions and once you stop forging chains that enslave you.